Dona Snipes
DRYBRUSHING SOFT SCULPTURE

For years, sewing enthusiasts have been making soft sculpture items with cloth and stuffing. Now, we ceramists can achieve the same look, too. The styling of the new molds and the greenware available today, combined with the drybrushing technique, have made this type of decorating possible. You won't have to worry about finding fabrics in just the right colors or designs; with a few jars of stain and the proper brushes, you can create fabric-like designs in any colors you choose. By following the techniques and instructions in this book, you will soon be painting ceramics that everyone will want to pinch!

Dona Snipes

DRYBRUSHING SOFT SCULPTURE

ISBN# 0-916809-13-7
Library of Congress - 86-060508
PRINTED IN U.S.A.

Copyright© 1986 Scott Publications
30595 W. 8 Mile Rd., Livonia, MI 48152

CONTENTS

PAGE
Drybrushing and Soft Sculpture Instructions: 6

Projects:

Turkey, Pumpkins, and Letters 9
Musical Pom-pom Teddy Bear Bank 11
Valentine Basket and Musical Bells 13
Musical Button Bunny 15
Butterfly Plaques 17
Pumpkin and Pumpkin Tray 18
Heart Box 19
Christmas Set 21
Kitten Box 23
Bunny Basket, Egg Box, and Bunnies 25
Duck Basket 27
Rocking Horse Lamp 29
Baby Block Musical Ornaments 30
Duck Planter, Eggs, and Little Ducks 31
Christmas Ornaments 33
Musical Pom-pom Bunny Bank 35
Musical Bells 37
Christmas Tree, Tray, and Small Bells 39

Musical Mementos:

Valentine Hearts 42
"Christmas Is" Hearts 43
Easter Eggs 44
Baby Girl 45
Baby Boy 45
Happy Father's Day 47
Happy Mother's Day 47
Birthday and Wedding Wishes 48

Drybrushing Soft Sculpture Basics:

I. Soft Sculpture: What it is:

Soft sculpture is the term used to describe cleaned, fired, and painted ceramic pieces that have been designed to resemble sewn and stuffed cloth items. The object is to finish these pieces, so that they look as soft and plush as if they had been made of fabric. The styling of the pieces pictured in this book, combined with the drybrushing technique, makes them appear to have been made on a sewing machine instead of at the painting table. You actually have to touch them to see that they are really **not** soft!

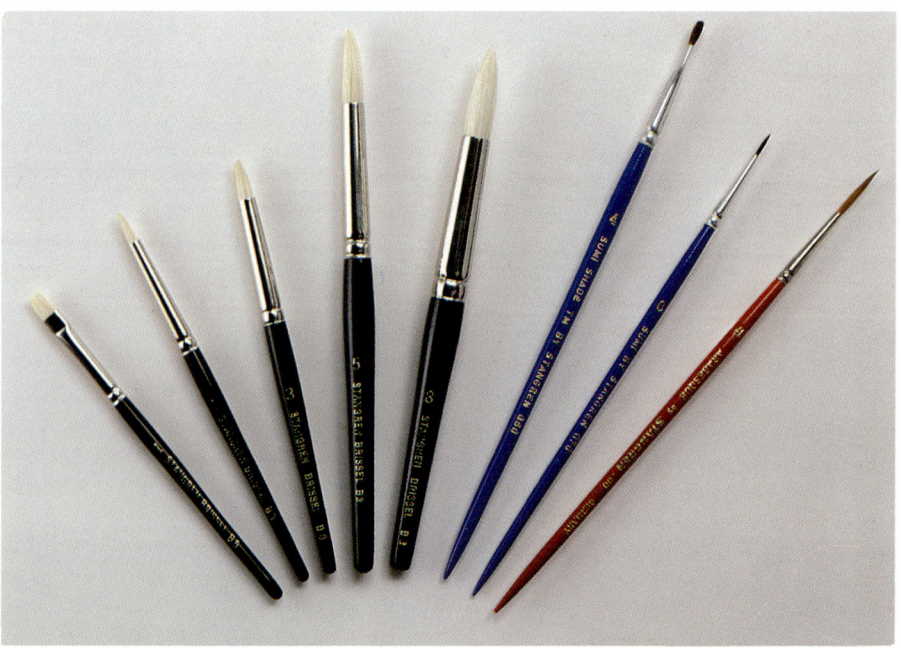

II. Drybrushing: What it is.

Drybrushing is the term used when applying a non-firing stain in light coats, slowly building up the color to the desired intensity on a bisque piece of ceramic which has been previously base coated and antiqued.

III. Types of Brushes to Use:

You must use stiff bristle brushes when applying the base coat colors and also for the actual drybrushing. Use flat or round bristle brushes in sizes one through eight (1-8), depending on the size of the area being colored. Always use the largest size brush that you can for the size of the area that you are working on.

If you use a paste antiquing, you will also need to use a stiff bristle brush in order to work the antiquing color into the crevices of the piece.

For doing the detail and design work required on the soft-sculpture pieces, you will need a variety of decorating brushes. A small Sumi (detail or feature) brush and a liner brush will be needed. For doing plaid designs, a square shader is required.

IV. Preparation of Greenware:

Every step in drybrushing has to be done carefully from the beginning, and the beginning is in cleaning the greenware. The pieces must be cleaned well and the details you may have removed in the cleaning process must be put back. Use a sgraffito tool or a stylus to recarve the details. The reason for this is that in drybrushing you will be brushing across the details of the piece and the paint will catch and build up on any raised area as well as any flaws and make it show up more, so cleaning is very important.

When cleaning a piece that is to be a bank, music box, or have a light fixture in it, be sure to make the correct holes or adjustments before firing. Fire the pieces to cone 06-05.

V. Selecting the Base Coat Color:

When selecting the color for the base coat, think of how you wish the finished project to look.

You will be using a mixture of two (2) parts of White to one (1) part of Smog Gray as the base coat on most of the lighter colored projects and Camel on the darker colored ones. As you will be using colored antiquing, these base coats will not appreciably change or distort the color of the antiquing.

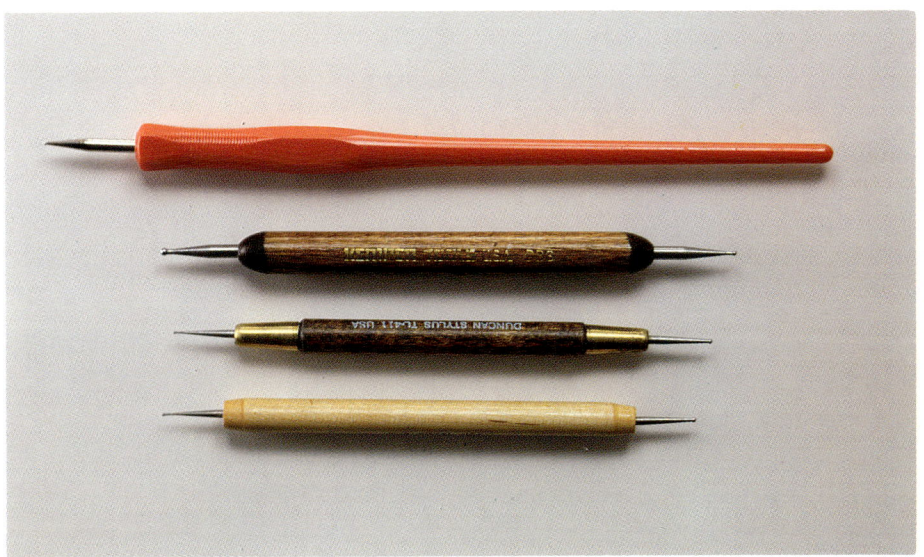

VI Applying the Base coats:

You **must** apply the base coats as smoothly as possible. Put very little color on your brush and brush it on smoothly, working it down into the creases of the bisque piece. If you apply too much of the base coat stain at one time, it will dry in thick ridges; these ridges will show up and spoil the appearance of the piece when you later do the drybrushing. Always apply two (2) coats of base coat color, applying the second coat in the *same* direction as the first coat; DO NOT crosshatch the coats of base coat color.

The two coats of base coat color can also be applied with an airbrush; this gives a nice smooth coverage and it is, of course, much faster.

VII Selecting the Color of Antiquing:

When selecting the antiquing for a soft-sculptured project, you must use a slightly darker color that is in the same color family as the colors you will be drybrushing over it. When the finished piece is to be pink, you will need to use pink antiquing in a slightly darker shade. The piece is supposed to look as much like cloth as possible. When you gather up a piece of pink material, the folds are still pink, only they are shadowed or darker than the other areas of the fabric.

Also, since most soft-sculptured pieces have large, smooth areas, the colored antiquing gives the piece some color and makes the coverage of these smooth areas much easier to accomplish.

VIII Applying the Antiquing:

Antique only a small area at a time, wiping it off with a piece of T-shirt material. Do not allow too much of the antiquing to build up in the crevices.

If you are doing pieces that are to match when finished, it is a good idea to antique all of them before you start to do the drybrushing.

Allow the antiquing to dry before starting to drybrush.

IX Drybrushing How to do it:

Using a bristle brush, tip it into the color, then brush it out on paper such as a grocery bag, so that very little color remains in the brush. Lightly brush the color on the desired area. In this manner, slowly build up the color by going over it until it is fairly even. When highlighting over a color or with a different tone — lighter or darker — you still want some of the original color to show. When highlighting with more than one color, use less of each succeeding color, so that *all* of the colors still show.

In addition to using opaque stains to drybrush, you can also use pearl stains to make a soft-sculptured piece look like satin material.

X Tools Used for Decorating:

The main tool to use in decorating the soft-sculptured pieces is the stylus. This is a tool with a tiny tip on the end. Many companies make these and they are all a little different in size, so they make a variety of sizes of dots. A stylus is used to make uniform sized dots. By making a series of dots, you can form flowers and many other designs, or make an overall pattern of dots for the effect of dotted-swiss material.

There are also many new design tools available. These are used to make slightly larger designs than are achieved with a stylus.

XI Decorating:

To make dots or dot flowers using a stylus, shake the jar of stain and remove the cover. Tip the end of the stylus into the stain remaining in the lid, then set the stylus onto the piece where you want a dot and lift it *straight* up. Set the stylus in the lid again and then onto the piece for each dot. Clean off the tip of the tool after every few dots to prevent the stain from building up on it and distorting the shape of the dots. If you make more than

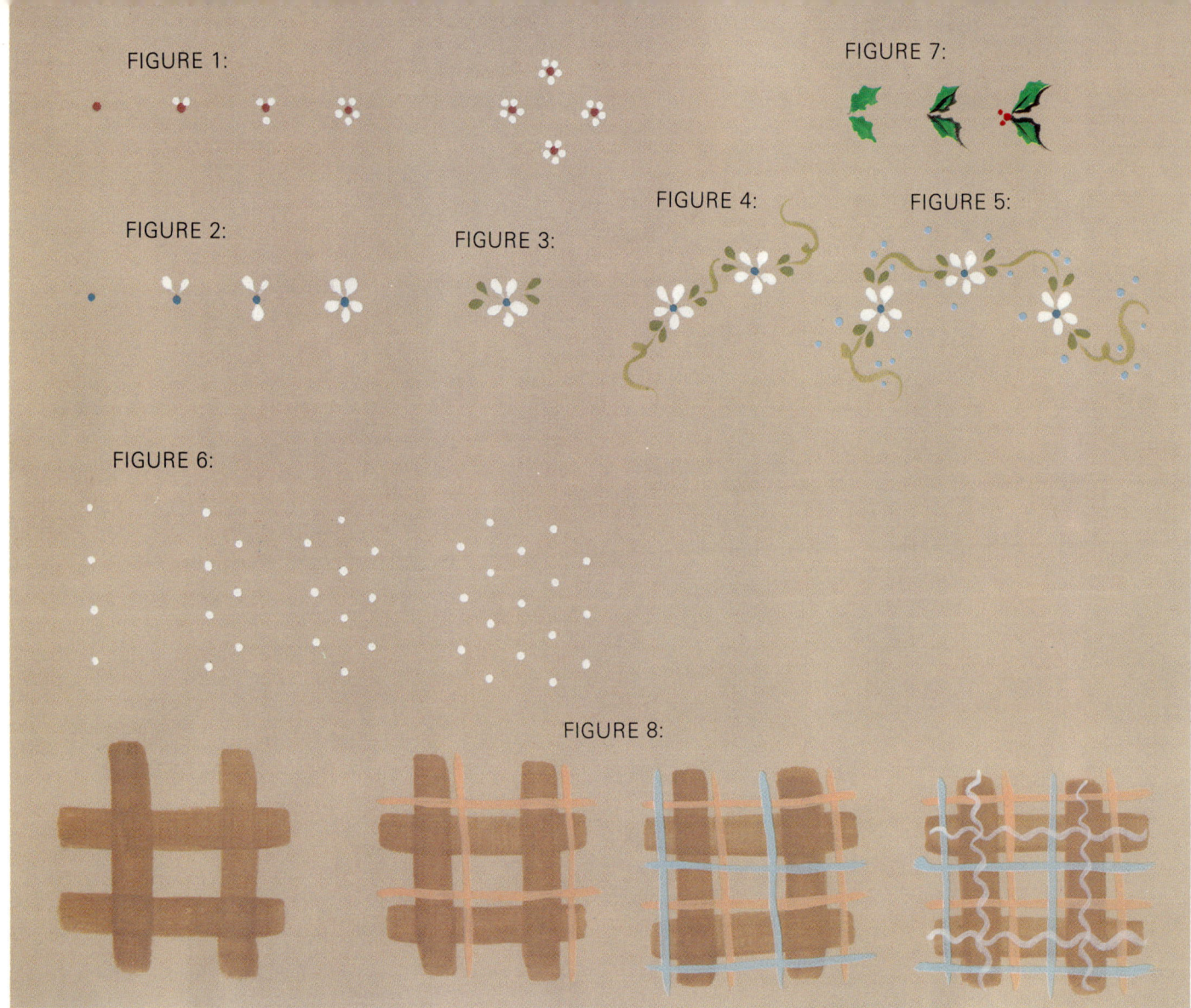

one dot before tipping the tool into the color, the dots will become progressively smaller. Be sure to practice on paper before applying the dots on a piece.

When making dot flowers (Figure 1), make all of the center dots on the area you are covering, then go back and put two (2) dots above each center dot. Next, put a dot under the center dot, centering it between the top ones, then finish the flower by adding a dot on each side. By applying the petal dots in this order, they will be evenly spaced.

The brush-print flowers (Figure 2) are done in the same manner. Make leaves by adding two more brush prints on each side of the flower (figure 3). By adding a wavy line between the flowers and a few dots in another color (Figures 4 & 5), you will end up with a dainty garland of flowers.

When doing an overall pattern (Figure 6) using a stylus, start by making one (1) row of dots across the area to be decorated. If you have trouble spacing the dots, cut a strip of lined notebook paper and lay it on the piece. Holding it tightly in place, make a dot on the *piece* at the end of each line on the paper. Do this only on the first row of dots to get you started, the next row of dots should be equally spaced *between* the dots of the first row.

XII Additional Accessories:

The addition of satin ribbon, silk flowers, and cotton pom-poms add to the soft sculptured look.

Please read through the technique before starting to paint! ∎

Turkey, Pumpkins, & Letters

MATERIALS LIST:
- Non-firing opaque stains: Camel, Russet, Bittersweet, Tobacco, Really Red, Flesh, Black, White, Butterscotch, Mustard, Buttercup, and Cordovan.
- Non-firing translucent stain: Copper Oak.
- Brush-on gloss sealer.
- Ribbon.
- Self-adhesive magnetic tape.
- Fine sandpaper.

When cleaning the greenware letters, the back of them must be flat so that the magnetic tape will adhere. To accomplish this, slide them back and forth on a piece of fine sandpaper until they are perfectly flat on the back.

Fire all pieces to cone 06-05.

Apply two (2) coats of Camel to all of the pieces. Antique with Copper Oak.

Step 1: Drybrush Tobacco on the stems of the pumpkins, the main part of the turkey's body, head, and on the edges of all of the letters. Lightly highlight with Butterscotch.

Step 2: Drybrush the turkey's beak with Mustard and lightly highlight it with Buttercup.

Step 3: Drybrush Really Red on the wattle.

Step 4: Referring to the color photo, drybrush Bittersweet on all of the darkest areas. Highlight with Russet.

Step 5: Drybrush Butterscotch on all of the lightest sections; highlight with Camel.

Step 6: Drybrush Russet on the remaining areas and highlight them with Butterscotch.

Step 7: Using a stylus, make tiny dots of Camel on the darkest areas.

Step 8: Make center dots for flowers of Cordovan on the lightest areas. Make five (5) dots of White around each Cordovan dot to form flowers (refer to Drybrushing and Soft Sculpture Basics: XI).

Step 9: On the remaining sections, make center dots of Really Red, then make five (5) dots of Bittersweet around each one to form a flower.

Step 10: Paint two (2) coats of White in the eyes. Make the irises Tobacco and the lashes Black. Paint a tiny White dot in each eye for a life light.

Step 11: Drybrush Flesh on the lace and highlight it with White.

Step 12: Tie a ribbon around the base of the tail feathers.

Step 13: Cut the strips of magnetic tape into small sections and fasten them to the backs of the letters. ∎

Musical Pom-pom Teddy Bear Bank

MATERIALS LIST:

- Non-firing opaque stains: White, Smog Gray, Butterscotch, Camel, Flesh, Turquoise, Ginger, Rose, Chocolate, and Black.
- Non-firing translucent stain: Golden Fawn.
- Brush-on gloss sealer.
- Ribbon.
- Glue.
- 2" pom-pom.
- "Touch-me" electronic music box (button only).

When cleaning the greenware, make a coin slot in the back of the hat. Fire to cone 06-05.

Base coat with a mixture of two (2) parts of White and one (1) part of Smog Gray. Antique with Golden Fawn.

Step 1: Drybrush White on the tummy, inside ear, pads on feet and paws, and the section around the tail.

Step 2: Drybrush Camel on the rest of the bear. Highlight all of the creases with Flesh.

Step 3: Tip the brush into Ginger and then into Rose and brush out well on paper, then apply this mixture lightly on the cheeks and a little heavier on the lip.

Step 4: Drybrush a little Turquoise above the eyes. Paint 3 coats of White on the eyes. Make the irises Chocolate and the pupils and lashes Black. Use Black for the nose. Paint a tiny White dot in the pupil of each eye for a life light.

Step 5: Make a mixture of equal parts of Turquoise and Flesh and drybrush it on the hat. Highlight the creases of the hat with Flesh.

Step 6: Using a stylus, make an overall dot pattern on the hat with White.

Step 7: Referring to Drybrushing and Soft Sculpture Basics: XI, use a #4 square shader brush to paint wide vertical and horizontal stripes of Butterscotch on the White areas. Mix equal parts of Ginger and Rose and, using a liner brush, paint a tiny line of this mixture *above* the horizontal stripes of Butterscotch and to the *right* of the vertical stripes. Then paint a tiny line of the Turquoise mixture (Step 5) to the *left* of the vertical stripes of Butterscotch and *under* the horizontal stripes. Paint a wavy line of White through the middle of all of the Butterscotch stripes.

Step 8: Apply two or three coats of brush-on gloss sealer on the eyes and nose.

Step 9: Tie a bow and glue it under the bear's chin.

Step 10: To make the musical pom-pom for the hat, apply glue to the *top plastic rim* of the "Touch-me" electronic music button (do not get glue on the metal center of the button), and center a 2" pom-pom on it and press around the edges. Apply glue to the four little tabs on the back of the button and press into place in the recessed area on the end of the hat. See small photo for details. ∎

Valentine Basket and Musical Bells

MATERIALS LIST:

- Non-firing opaque stains: Fuchsia, Mauve, Plum, Rose, White, and Smog Gray.
- Non-firing metallic translucent stain: Ruby-glo.
- Ribbon.
- Small silk flowers.
- Floral foam.
- Wood flower picks.
- Glue.
- 2" "Touch-me" electronic music boxes (for bells).

Base coat all of the pieces with a mixture of two (2) parts White and one (1) part Smog Gray. Antique all of the pieces with Ruby-glo.

Step 1: Drybrush White on all lace and on the bell loops. Go over the lace several times, slowly building up the White, so that you do not fill in the holes and creases.

Step 2: Referring to the color photo, drybrush Fuchsia on the darkest areas. Since this is such a dark color, it will be necessary to go over it several times, making it almost solid. Highlight the Fuchsia areas with Mauve. Using a stylus, make tiny White dots, spaced evenly on these sections.

Step 3: Drybrush Plum on the lightest areas; lightly highlight the same areas with Rose. Use a stylus to make center dots for the flowers with Mauve. Make the dot petals (5 dots around each Mauve dot) with Rose.

Step 4: Drybrush Mauve on the remaining areas and highlight with Plum. Make the flower center dots in these sections with Fuchsia and the five petal dots around each one with White.

Step 5: Glue an electronic "Touch-me" music box cup in the bottom of each bell. Apply glue to the music box buttons and attach one to each cup. Allow to dry.

Step 6: Tie bows around the loops on the bell tops and on the basket handle.

Step 7: Glue a piece of floral foam into the bottom of the basket and arrange the silk flowers on it.

Step 8: Glue the wooden flower picks into the small pour holes in the backs of the little hearts. Allow the glue to dry, then place the hearts in the basket. ■

Musical Button Bunny

MATERIALS LIST:
- Non-firing opaque stains: White, Smog Gray, Rose, Soft Pink, Flamingo, Flesh, Chocolate, Black, Moss, Ginger, Buttercup, and Turquoise.
- Non-firing translucent stain: Pink Crystal.
- Non-firing metallic stain: Silver.
- Brush-on gloss sealer.
- Ribbon.
- Glue.
- "Touch-me" electronic music box (button only).

The greenware basket and the cup that fits inside of it should be poured thin, so that the bunny will sit down in the cup far enough. When cleaning the greenware, be sure that you DO NOT clean off the rim on the bottom of the bunny; this rim should be flat (carefully stand up the bunny to make sure it is). The music button will be glued inside to the bottom of the inner cup that the bunny sits in. The rim on the bottom of the bunny rests on the metal center of the music button. When you push down on the bunny's head, it starts the music box.

Fire to cone 06-05.

Base coat the pieces with a mixture of two (2) parts of White and one (1) part of Smog Gray. Antique with Pink Crystal.

Step 1: Referring to the color photo, drybrush White on the main parts of the bunny and on the wood rim at the top of the basket.

Step 2: Drybrush Rose in the ears, on the chest, and on the bottom of the basket. Highlight with Soft Pink and then lightly with Flesh.

Step 3: Drybrush Ginger on the nose and lightly on the cheeks; highlight both with Rose.

Step 4: Drybrush Buttercup on the straw and highlight with Flesh.

Step 5: Drybrush Turquoise above the eyes. Paint the eyes with two coats of White. Make the irises Chocolate and the pupils and lashes Black. Paint a tiny White dot in each eye for a life light.

Step 6: Using a stylus, make tiny White dots on the snout, backs of ears, and the inside panels on the arms.

Step 7: Paint tiny White flowers on the basket bottom, chest, and insides of ears (refer to Drybrushing and Soft Sculpture Basics: XI). Use Flamingo for the flower centers and Moss for the leaves. Make tiny White dots on the background of these areas.

Step 8: Paint metallic Silver on the staples on the wood band.

Step 9: Paint two (2) coats of brush-on gloss sealer on the eyes and nose.

Step 10: Glue the music box button to the inside bottom of the inner cup.

Step 11: Tie 2 bows and glue one to the front of the basket and the other to the top of the bunny's head. ■

Butterfly Plaques

MATERIALS LIST:
- ☐ Non-firing opaque stains: White, Smog Gray, Turquoise, Peacock, and Flesh.
- ☐ Non-firing translucent stain: Aqua Sheen.
- ☐ Ribbon.
- ☐ Glue.

Mix two (2) parts of White to one (1) part of Smog Gray and apply two coats of this mixture to each piece. Antique with Aqua Sheen.

Before starting to drybrush, mix some colors for the additional tones of Turquoise, as follows: Mix equal parts of Turquoise and Flesh for a light tone. Mix two (2) parts of Peacock to one (1) part of Turquoise for a dark Turquoise tone.

Step 1: Drybrush White on the heads, body sections, and on the edges of all wings.

Step 2: Referring to the color photo, drybrush the Dark Turquoise mixture on the darkest sections of the wings; highlight with Turquoise.

Step 3: Drybrush the Light Turquoise mixture on the lightest sections of the wings; highlight with Flesh.

Step 4: Drybrush the remaining sections of the wings with Turquoise and highlight with the Light Turquoise mixture.

Step 5: Using a stylus, make tiny White dots on the White edges and the middle body sections.

Step 6: Make flower center dots on the darkest sections with the Dark Turquoise mixture. Make five (5) flower petals around each dot with the Light Turquoise mixture.

Step 7: On the lightest sections, make flower center dots of Turquoise and five (5) petal dots of White.

Step 8: On the remaining sections, make flower center dots with White. Make five (5) flower petal dots with the Dark Turquoise mixture.

Step 9: Tie three small bows and glue one to the bottom of each head section. ■

Pumpkin and Pumpkin Tray

MATERIALS LIST:
- Non-firing opaque stains: Camel, White, Black, Bittersweet, Russet, Cordovan, Tobacco, and Butterscotch.
- Non-firing translucent stain: Black.
- Glaze.

After cleaning and firing the greenware, the bisque pumpkin and lid and fire again to cone 06-05.

Apply two (2) coats of Camel to all of the pieces and antique with Black translucent stain.

Step 1: Drybrush Bittersweet on every other panel on the pumpkin and on one of the leaves on each piece. Lightly highlight with Russet.

Step 2: Drybrush Russet on the remaining panels and leaves. Lightly highlight with Butterscotch.

Step 3: Drybrush Cordovan on the stems and highlight with Tobacco.

Step 4: Highlight the edges of the stems and leaves with Butterscotch.

Step 5: Paint the stitches in the veins of the Russet leaves with Bittersweet. Paint the veins of the Bittersweet leaves with Russet.

Step 6: Make White dots for the centers of the flowers on the Russet panels, then make five (5) dots of Bittersweet around each White dot to form the flowers. Make Black dots randomly between the flowers.

Step 7: On the Bittersweet panels of the pumpkin, make Black dots for the flower centers. Make five (5) dots of Russet around each Black dot to form the flower. Randomly make White dots between the flowers. ■

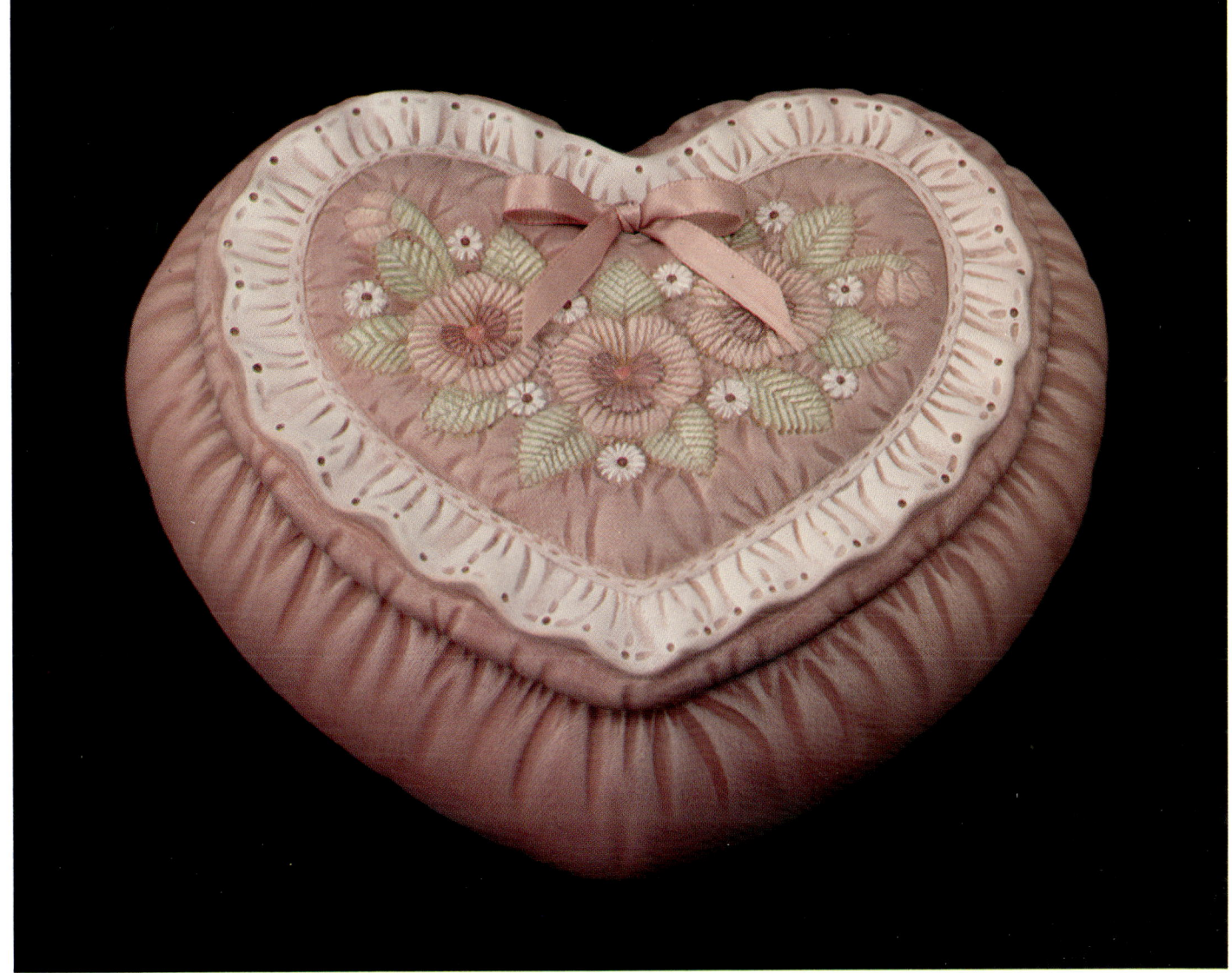

Heart Box

MATERIALS LIST:
- Non-firing opaque stains: White, Mauve, Fuchsia, Plum, Rose, Flamingo, Flesh, Moss, Mint, and Smog Gray.
- Non-firing translucent stain: Ruby-glo.
- Pink glaze.
- Ribbon.
- Glue.

After cleaning and firing the greenware to cone 06-05, glaze the inside of the lid and the box with Pink glaze and fire to cone 06-05.

Mix two (2) parts of White to one (1) part of Smog Gray and apply two coats of the mixture to the bisque areas of both pieces. Antique with Ruby-glo.

Step 1: Drybrush the entire box and the background of the lid with Mauve, building up this color until it is fairly solid. Highlight with Plum, then lightly highlight the edges where the creases are with Rose.

Step 2: Drybrush White on the lace and on the tiny flowers.

Step 3: Drybrush the inner petals on the large flowers with Mauve and highlight them with Flamingo. Drybrush the outer petals with Plum and highlight them with Rose.

Step 4: Solidly paint the centers of the large flowers with Flamingo and the centers of the small ones with Fuchsia.

Step 5: Drybrush the leaves with Moss. With the Moss still on the tip of the brush, tip into Mint and highlight with this mixture.

Step 6: Lightly highlight over all of the flowers and leaves with Flesh.

Step 7: Tie a bow and glue it on top of the box lid. ∎

Christmas Set

MATERIALS LIST:

☐ Non-firing opaque stains: White, Smog Gray, Fuchsia, Mauve, Plum, Rose, Black, and Melon.
☐ Non-firing translucent stain: Ruby-glo.
☐ Brush-on gloss sealer.
☐ Ribbon.
☐ Silk flowers and pearl sprigs.
☐ One ornament hook.
☐ Three small bells (for clappers
    in the bells).
☐ Glue.

When cleaning the pieces, make a small hole in the top of the tree (for later attaching the ornament hook to hold the bow), and a hole in the top of each bell. Cut out the top part of the saddle on the hobbyhorse for a flower arrangement. Fire all of the pieces to cone 06-05.

Base coat all of the pieces with a mixture of two (2) parts of White and one (1) part of Smog Gray. Antique with Ruby-glo.

TREE, TRAY, AND BELLS:

Step 1: Drybrush White on all lace.

Step 2: Referring to the color photo, drybrush Fuchsia on all of the darkest areas. Build this color up until it is fairly solid. Highlight with Mauve. Decorate these sections with an allover pattern of White dots.

Step 3: Drybrush the lightest areas with Plum and lightly highlight with Rose. On these

TO PAGE 40

Kitten Box

MATERIALS LIST:
- ☐ Non-firing opaque stains: White, Smog Gray, Rose, Plum, Ginger, Chocolate, Black and Flesh.
- ☐ Non-firing translucent stain: Pink Crystal.
- ☐ Non-firing metallic Silver stain.
- ☐ Brush-on gloss sealer.
- ☐ Glaze.

After cleaning and firing the greenware, glaze the inside of the box and lid and fire again to cone 06-05.

Base coat all pieces with a mixture of two (2) parts of White and one (1) part of Smog Gray. Antique with Pink Crystal.

Step 1: Drybrush Rose on the quilted top of the lid, the front panel, the two side back panels of the box bottom; the kittens' paws, ears, snouts, and the top section of the tails. Lightly highlight all of these areas with Flesh.

Step 2: Drybrush Plum on the wood rim around the top of the box lid and on the kittens' bows. Lightly highlight with Rose.

Step 3: Drybrush White on the remaining areas on the kittens, the lace around the lid, and the remaining panels on the box.

Step 4: Drybrush Ginger on the kittens' cheeks, then leaving the Ginger on the brush, tip into Rose and highlight the cheeks. If you should get the cheeks too dark, tip into a little White and brush this out on paper, then softly go over the areas.

Step 5: Drybrush Plum on the kittens' noses and highlight with Ginger.

Step 6: Paint two (2) coats of White in all of the eyes. Make the irises Chocolate and the pupils and lashes Black. Paint a tiny White dot in each eye for a life light.

Step 7: Apply two (2) coats of metallic Silver on the screw on the back of the lid.

Step 8: Apply two (2) coats of brush-on gloss sealer on the eyes and noses.

Step 9: Using a stylus, make tiny White dots on the Rose panels of the box bottom and on the Rose areas of the kittens.

Step 10: Make Rose dots for the flower centers on the White panels of the box and use White for the petals. Make Plum dots between the flowers. ■

Bunny Basket, Egg Box, and Bunnies

MATERIALS LIST:
- Non-firing opaque stains: White, Turquoise, Rose, Ginger, Moss, Flesh, Chocolate, Black, and Smog Gray.
- Non-firing translucent stain: Aqua Sheen.
- Brush-on gloss sealer.
- Ribbon.
- Silk flowers.
- Glue.
- Small cotton pom-poms (optional).
- Glaze.

When cleaning these pieces, make holes in the small bunnies' hands to hold silk flowers. If you wish to use the cotton pom-poms for tails, cut off the greenware tails. Fire all of the pieces to cone 06-05.

Glaze the inside of the egg box and fire it to cone 06-05.

Base coat all of the pieces with a mixture of two (2) parts of White and one (1) part of Smog Gray. Antique with Aqua Sheen.

Step 1: Referring to the color photo, drybrush White on all of the bunnies, on the lightest areas of the eggs, basket, and on the lace.

Step 2: Drybrush Rose inside all of the bunnies' ears and on the bottom pads of the feet.

Step 3: Drybrush the darkest areas with Turquoise. Make a mixture of equal parts of Turquoise and Flesh and use it to highlight over the Turquoise. Using a stylus, make White dots on these sections.

Step 4: Drybrush the light Turquoise mixture from the previous step on the remaining areas of all pieces. Highlight this with Flesh. Paint small White flowers in these areas. Paint a dot of Rose in each flower center. Make the leaves Moss.

Step 5: Drybrush Ginger on the noses and lightly on the cheeks. Highlight the cheeks with a little Rose.

Step 6: Drybrush a little Turquoise above the eyes. Paint two (2) coats of White in the eyes. Make the irises Chocolate. Use Black for the pupils and lashes. Paint a tiny dot of White in all eyes for a life light.

Step 7: Paint two (2) coats of brush-on gloss sealer on all eyes and noses.

Step 8: Tie large bows on each side of the basket handle. Tie small bows and glue them on the little bunnies, including the back of the neck of the bunny on the basket handle.

Step 9: If you removed the greenware tails from the bunnies, glue a pom-pom for a tail on each one.

Step 10: Glue the small eggs in the basket and place silk flowers between them. Glue small flowers in the bunnies' hands. ∎

Duck Basket

MATERIALS LIST:
- Non-firing opaque stains: White, Smog Gray, Buttercup, Blond, Flesh, Ginger, Melon, Pumpkin, Chocolate, Black, and Turquoise.
- Non-firing translucent stain: Peach-glo.
- Ribbon.
- Silk flowers.
- Glue.

Base coat the pieces with a mixture of two (2) parts of White and one (1) part of Smog Gray. Antique with Peach-glo.

Step 1: Referring to the color photo, drybrush Buttercup on the duck and the yellow sections of the basket and eggs. Highlight with Blond, then lightly with Flesh. Make the flower dot centers Ginger and the petal dots White. DO NOT put flowers on the duck.

Step 2: Drybrush White on the lace, the two side panels of the basket, and the white sections of the handle and eggs. Decorate these sections with groups of three (3) dots of Buttercup.

Step 3: Drybrush Ginger on the remaining sections of the basket and eggs. Lightly highlight with Flesh. Make White dots in these areas.

Step 4: Drybrush Ginger on the duck's feet and bill. Tip the brush into Pumpkin and a touch of Melon and highlight this on the feet and bill, then lightly highlight Flesh on the wrinkles.

Step 5: Lightly drybrush Ginger on the cheeks, then highlight them with a tiny bit of Melon.

Step 6: Lightly drybrush Turquoise above the eyes. Paint the eyes with two (2) coats of White, then make the irises Chocolate and the pupils and lashes Black. Paint a tiny dot of White in each eye for a life light.

Step 7: Tie bows on both sides of the basket handle.

Step 8: Glue the eggs in the basket and place silk flowers between them. ■

Rocking Horse Lamp

MATERIALS LIST:
- Non-firing opaque stains: White, Rose, Soft Pink, Plum, Flamingo, Chocolate, Black, Ginger, and Melon.
- Non-firing translucent stain: Pink Crystal.
- Brush-on gloss sealer.
- Ribbon.
- Silk flowers.
- Lamp fixture.
- Floral foam.

SPECIAL INSTRUCTIONS:
After cleaning the greenware horse and separate rocker base, make a hole in the top of the saddle and one in the base for the lamp rod; be sure that these holes line up. Also, put a small hole in the base for the electric cord. Cut a kidney-shaped opening in each side of the saddle for the flower arrangements. Fire the pieces to cone 06-05.

Base coat both pieces with Soft Pink. Antique with Pink Crystal.

Step 1: Drybrush White on the mane, tail, feet, and saddle.

Step 2: Referring to the color photo, drybrush Rose on the plain areas of the horse and on the quilted part of the rocker base. With the Rose still on the brush, tip into Flamingo and lightly highlight the quilted lines of the base and the tucks on the Rose sections of the horse.

Step 3: On the remaining sections of the horse, lightly drybrush with Soft Pink. Using a stylus, make tiny White dots on these areas.

Step 4: Referring to Drybrushing and Soft Sculpture Basics: XI, paint Rose flowers on the feet and saddle. Make dots of Flamingo in the flower centers. Use Moss for the leaves. Make a sprinkle of tiny White dots between the flowers.

Step 5: Solidly paint the buttons with Plum and use White for the stitches.

Step 6: Tip the brush into Ginger and a tiny bit of Melon, brush out on paper, and apply lightly on the horse's cheeks.

Step 7: Paint two (2) or three (3) coats of White on the eyes. Make the irises Chocolate and the pupils and lashes Black. Paint a tiny White dot in each pupil for a life light.

Step 8: Paint two (2) coats of brush-on gloss sealer on the buttons and eyes.

Step 9: Tie two (2) bows and glue one on the front of the mane and one on the base of the tail.

Step 10: Install the lamp fixture.

Step 11: Put floral foam in the openings on the saddle and arrange the flowers. ■

Baby Block Musical Ornaments

MATERIALS LIST:
- Non-firing opaque stains: White, Smog Gray, Mint, Turquoise, Rose, and Flesh.
- Non-firing translucent stains: Lime Lite and Holly Brite.
- Non-firing pearl stains: Mint, Rose, White, and Aqua.
- 2 ornament hooks.
- Ribbon.
- 2 "Touch-me" electronic music boxes.

After cleaning the greenware blocks, check to make sure that the music boxes will fit. Make a tiny hole in the top of each block. Fire the pieces to cone 06-05

Base coat the blocks with a mixture of two (2) parts of White and one (1) part of Smog Gray.

For the antiquing, mix 1/2 teaspoonful of Holly Brite and a full jar of Lime Lite. Mix thoroughly.

GIRL BLOCK:

Step 1: Drybrush Mint on the top, bottom, and edges of the block.

Step 2: Drybrush Rose on the background of all sides.

Step 3: Drybrush Turquoise on the large letters on the sides and on the carriage blanket.

Step 4: Lightly highlight all with Flesh.

Step 5: Using a stylus, make tiny White dots on the letters and blanket.

Step 6: Drybrush Mint on the holly leaves, then apply two (2) coats of Mint pearl.

Step 7: Paint two (2) coats of Rose pearl on the holly berries.

Step 8: Drybrush White on the carriage. Paint two (2) coats of White pearl on the carriage handle, wheels, and the edge of the blanket.

BOY BLOCK:

Step 1: Drybrush Mint on the top, bottom, and edges of the block.

TO PAGE 40

Duck Planter, Eggs, and Little Ducks

MATERIALS LIST:
- Non-firing opaque stains: White, Smog Gray, Buttercup, Blond, Flesh, Ginger, Melon, Pumpkin, Chocolate, Black, Moss, and Turquoise.
- Non-firing translucent stain: Peach-glo.
- Non-firing metallic stain: Silver.
- Brush-on gloss sealer.
- Ribbon.
- Floral foam.
- Silk flowers.
- Wooden flower picks.
- Glue.
- Silver cord.

When cleaning these pieces, be sure to put holes in the wood rim for the cord on the handle to go through, a hole through the handle, and in the wings of the little ducks for the flowers (refer to the color photo). Fire all pieces to cone 06-05.

Base coat the pieces with a mixture of two (2) parts of White and one (1) part of Smog Gray. Antique with Peach-glo.

Step 1: Drybrush Buttercup on the ducks' heads, bodies, and wings. Highlight with Blond, then lightly with Flesh on the creases.

Step 2: Drybrush White on the tummy and tail sections, and on the wood handle and rim of the basket.

Step 3: Drybrush Ginger on the basket bottom and the ducks' feet and bills. Highlight the feet and bills with Pumpkin. With the Pumpkin still in the brush, tip into a little Melon and lightly highlight with this mixture. Drybrush Flesh on the wrinkles of the basket and on the edges of the bills and feet of the ducks.

Step 4: Drybrush Turquoise above the eyes for eye shadow. Paint two (2) or three (3) coats of White on the eyes

TO PAGE 40

Christmas Ornaments

MATERIALS LIST:
- Non-firing opaque stains: White, Smog Gray, Mint, Shamrock, Really Red, Flesh and Black.
- Non-firing translucent stains: Lime Lite and Holly Brite.
- Ribbon.

Base coat all pieces with a mixture of two (2) parts of White and one (1) part of Smog Gray.

For the antiquing, mix 1/2 teaspoonful of Holly Brite with one jarful of Lime Lite; mix thoroughly.

Step 1: Referring to the color photo, drybrush White on all of the lace and the areas that have the holly print on them.

Step 2: Drybrush Mint on the lightest green areas and highlight with Flesh.

Step 3: Do not drybrush any additional color on the remaining sections. Use a stylus to make an allover pattern of White dots on these areas.

Step 4: Trace the holly pattern (see Drybrushing and Soft Sculpture Basics: XI) and transfer it on the White panels. Solidly paint the leaves with Shamrock. Mix a bit of Black with some Shamrock and use it to outline the bottom edges of the leaves and for the center veins. Use a stylus and Really Red stain to make three (3) berries above each pair of leaves.

Step 5: Tie a ribbon on each ornament. ■

Musical Pom-pom Bunny Bank

MATERIALS LIST:
- Non-firing opaque stains: White, Smog Gray, Copenhagen, Baby Blue, Ginger, Rose, and Black.
- Non-firing translucent stain: Golden Dusk.
- Brush-on gloss sealer.
- Glue.
- "Touch-me" electronic music box (button only).
- 2" pom-pom
- Electronic musical bank slot (optional).
- Ribbon.

When cleaning this piece, you can make a regular coin slot, or you can enlarge the slot to hold a musical bank slot. Fire the piece to cone 06-05.

Base coat with a mixture of two (2) parts of White and one (1) part of Smog Gray. Antique with Golden Dusk.

Step 1: Referring to the color photo, drybrush Copenhagen on all of the darkest areas. Highlight these areas with a mixture of two (2) parts of Baby Blue and one (1) part of Copenhagen.

Step 2: Drybrush White on the tummy, inside panels of ears, and bottom sections of feet.

Step 3: Tip the brush into Ginger and then into Rose and brush out well on paper. Lightly apply this mixture to the cheeks.

Step 4: Drybrush the remaining areas with the Baby Blue-Copenhagen mixture used in Step 1. Using a stylus, make an overall pattern of White dots on these same areas.

Step 5: Paint three (3) coats of White on the eyes. Paint the irises Copenhagen and the pupils and lashes Black. Paint a tiny White dot in each pupil.

Step 6: Apply two (2) coats of brush-on gloss sealer to the eyes and nose.

Step 7: Referring to Figure 8, Drybrushing and Soft Sculpture Basics: XI, use a square shader brush to paint wide stripes of the Baby Blue Copenhagen mixture in both directions on all of the White areas. To the *right* of the vertical stripes and *under* the horizontal stripes, use a liner brush to paint a thin stripe of Copenhagen. Once again using the liner brush, paint a thin line of Ginger to the *left* of the wide vertical stripes and *above* the horizontal ones. Use the liner brush and White to paint a wavy line in the middle of the horizontal and vertical Copenhagen stripes.

Step 8: If you are going to use the musical bank slot, paint the top part of it with two (2) coats of Copenhagen. Allow the piece to dry, then glue it into the opening on the back of the head.

Step 9: To make the musical pom-pom tail, apply glue to the *top plastic rim* of the "Touch-me" electronic music box button and center a 2" pom-pom on it and press around the edges; allow to dry. Apply glue to the four little tabs on the bottom of the button and center this into the recessed tail area and allow to dry. To start the music, just push on the tail.

Step 10: Tie a bow and glue it under the bunny's chin. ■

Musical Bells

MATERIALS LIST:

- Non-firing opaque stains: White, Smog Gray, Buttercup, Blond, Ginger, and Flesh.
- Non-firing translucent stain: Peach-glo.
- Two (2) "Touch-me" electronic music boxes.
- Ribbon.
- Glue.

Base coat the bells with a mixture of two (2) parts of White and one (1) part of Smog Gray. Antique with Peach-glo.

Step 1: Referring to the color photo, drybrush Ginger on the peach colored sections, then lightly highlight with Flesh. Decorate these areas with groups of three (3) Buttercup dots.

Step 2: Drybrush Buttercup on the yellow areas; highlight with Blond and then lightly with Flesh. For the flowers on these sections, use Ginger for the center dots and White for the petals.

Step 3: Drybrush the remaining areas White. Work carefully, so that you do not build up the White too much, as these areas will be decorated with White dots; if the background is built up too much, the dots will not show. Use the stylus to apply the White dots.

Step 4: Drybrush White on the loops on top of the bells and on the lace.

Step 5: Tie bows around the loops.

Step 6: Glue the music box cups into the bottoms of the bells and glue the music box buttons to the cups. ■

Christmas Tree, Tray, and Small Bells

MATERIALS LIST:

- Non-firing opaque stains: White, Smog Gray, Mint, Shamrock, Moss, Spring Green, Really Red, and Flesh.
- Non-firing translucent stains: Lime Lite and Holly Brite.
- Non-firing pearl stain: Mint.
- Ribbon.
- Ornament hook.
- Three small bells (clappers for bells).

When cleaning these pieces, make a small hole in the top of the tree and a hole in the top of each bell. Fire all of the pieces to cone 06-05.

Base coat all pieces with a mixture of two (2) parts White and one (1) part Smog Gray.

For the antiquing, mix 1/2 teaspoonful of Holly Brite with one jarful of Lime Lite. Mix thoroughly.

Step 1: Drybrush White on all of the lace.

Step 2: Referring to the color photo, drybrush Moss on all of the darkest sections. Highlight with Spring Green; the Spring Green should show most, the Moss under it just tones down the color. Decorate these areas with White dots.

Step 3: Drybrush Mint on the lightest sections, then lightly highlight with Flesh. For the flowers on these sections, use Really Red for the centers and White dots for the petals. Paint two (2) small brush-print leaves on each side of the flowers.

Step 4: Referring to the color photo, drybrush the remaining sections on the bells with Mint pearl.

Step 5: Insert an ornament hook into the hole in the top of the tree and tie a bow on it.

Step 6: Tie a jingle bell on the middle of a ten (10) inch piece of narrow ribbon. Hold both ends and tie a knot about three (3) inches up from the jingle bell. Push the two ribbon ends through the hole in the top of the bell from the inside and tie a bow on top of the bell with the ribbon ends. Trim the ends. ∎

CHRISTMAS SET
FROM PAGE 21

sections, make Mauve center dots and Rose petal dots.

Step 4: Drybrush the remaining areas with Mauve and highlight with Plum. For the flowers on these sections, use Fuchsia for the center dots and White for the petal dots.

Step 5: Insert the ornament hook into the hole in the top of the tree. Tie a bow and attach it to the hook.

Step 6: To make the clappers for the bells, tie a little metal jingle bell in the middle of a ten (10) inch piece of narrow ribbon. Hold both ends and tie a knot about three (3) inches up from the jingle bell. Push the two ends of the ribbon through the hole in the top of the bell from the inside, then tie a bow on the top of the bell with the ends of the ribbon. Trim the ends.

HOBBYHORSE AND ROCKER BASE:

Step 1: Drybrush White on the saddle, lace, mane, buttons, and feet.

Step 2: Drybrush all of the darkest areas on the horse with Fuchsia and highlight with Mauve. Decorate these sections with an allover pattern of White dots.

Step 3: Drybrush Plum on the lightest sections of the horse and on the sides of the rocker base. Lightly highlight with Rose. Make dot flowers on these sections, using Mauve for the center dots and Rose for the petal dots.

Step 4: Drybrush the remaining areas on the horse and the quilted part of the rocker base with Mauve; highlight with Plum. For the flowers on these sections, make the center dots with Fuchsia and the petal dots White. DO NOT put flowers on the quilted section of the rocker base.

Step 5: Paint the rims of the buttons with White and use Fuchsia for the stitches.

Step 6: *Very lightly* drybrush Melon on the cheeks.

Step 7: Paint two (2) or three (3) coats of White on the eyes. Make the irises Mauve and the pupils and lashes Black. Paint a tiny White dot in each eye for a life light.

Step 8: Apply two (2) coats of brush-on gloss sealer on the eyes and buttons.

Step 9: Glue the horse to the rocker base.

Step 10: Tie two bows and glue one on the front of the horse's mane and the other one on the base of the tail.

Step 11: Put floral foam into the opening of the saddle and arrange silk flowers on it. ■

DUCK PLANTER, EGGS & LITTLE DUCKS
FROM PAGE 31

Make the irises Chocolate and the pupils and lashes Black. Paint a tiny White dot in each eye for a life light.

Step 5: Using a stylus, make White dots on the tummy and tail sections.

Step 6: Paint the staples with two (2) coats of metallic Silver.

Step 7: Using a feature brush, paint tiny White flowers on the basket bottom (Drybrushing and Soft Sculpture Basics - XI). Paint leaves with Moss. Mix a little Melon with Ginger for a darker shade of Ginger for the center dots in the flowers.

Step 8: Using a little of this same mixture, lightly drybrush the cheeks.

Step 9: Paint two (2) coats of brush-on gloss sealer on the eyes.

Step 10: String the silver cord through the handle and tie it on the basket.

Step 11: Tie small bows and glue them on the ducks' necks.

Step 12: Glue floral foam in the basket and arrange the silk flowers on it.

Step 13: Glue wooden flower picks in the pouring holes in the eggs. Allow the glue to dry, then place the eggs in the arrangement.

Step 14: Glue tiny flowers in the little ducks' wings. ■

BABY BLOCKS
FROM PAGE 45

Step 2: Drybrush Turquoise on the background on all sides.

Step 3: Drybrush Rose on the large letters on the sides.

Step 4: Lightly highlight all with Flesh.

Step 5: Using a stylus, make White dots on the letters.

Step 6: Drybrush Mint on the holly leaves, then apply two (2) coats of Mint pearl.

Step 7: Paint two (2) coats of Rose pearl on the holly berries.

Step 8: Drybrush White on the handles, tops, and bottoms of the rattles, then paint a coat of White pearl on the tops and bottoms. Drybrush Rose on the center bands of the rattles.

Step 9: Paint Aqua pearl on the knobs on the handles and on the buttons on the top of the rattles.

FINISHING:

Put an ornament hook in the hole in the top of each block and tie a ribbon on it.

Glue a music box cup in the opening in the bottom of each block, then glue the music button to the cup. ■

Musical Mementos

All of the small, soft-sculptured pieces on the following pages hold electronic "Touch-me" music box buttons (the caps are not used). These pieces make wonderful gifts for that someone special, and are also unique package tie-ons.

When cleaning the greenware for these pieces, be sure to clean the pour hole in the back of each one to fit the music box button, making sure to keep the hole as round as possible, so that the finished piece will look neat on the back. In addition, put a small hole in the top inside edge of the lace for a ribbon. ∎

Valentine Hearts

MATERIALS LIST:
- Non-firing opaque stains: White, Smog Gray, Plum, Rose, Moss, Mauve, Fuchsia, and Flamingo.
- Non-firing translucent stains: Ruby-glo and Pink Crystal.
- Non-firing pearl stain: Rose.
- Tiny silk flowers.
- Ribbon.
- Glue.
- Three (3) "Touch-me" electronic music box buttons.

Base coat the hearts with a mixture of two (2) parts of White and one (1) part of Smog Gray.

I LOVE YOU HEART:
Antique with Pink Crystal.
Drybrush White on the lace. Drybrush the background with Plum and highlight it with Rose. Drybrush Moss on the leaves. Drybrush the flowers with Mauve and highlight with Plum, then with a little Rose. Using a feature brush, paint tiny lines of Fuchsia radiating from the center outward on the two side petals. Paint White in the centers on the edges of the bottom petal.

PLAIN HEART:
Antique with Ruby-glo.
Drybrush White on the lace. Drybrush Mauve on the front and back, then highlight with Plum, then lightly around the edges with a little Rose. Make the center dot for each flower with Fuchsia and the five (5) petal dots with Rose.
When tying on the ribbon, put two little flowers in the knot.

BE MY VALENTINE HEART:
Antique with Ruby-glo.
Drybrush the lace with White. Drybrush the background with Mauve and highlight with Plum. Drybrush the leaves with Moss. Referring to the color photo, drybrush the darker flowers with Flamingo. Paint tiny Fuchsia lines radiating from the centers of all petals. Drybrush the remaining flowers with Plum and highlight them with Rose. Paint tiny lines of Fuchsia radiating outward on the two side petals. Paint White lines on the edge of the bottom petal toward the center. Paint the centers of all of the flowers White. Paint the tiny hearts with Fuchsia and then with Rose pearl. ∎

"Christmas Is" Hearts

MATERIALS LIST:
- Non-firing opaque stains: White, Smog Gray, Mint, Spring Green, Turquoise, Plum, Rose, Flesh, and Peacock.
- Non-firing translucent stains: Lime Lite, Holly Brite, Pink Crystal, and Aqua Sheen.
- Non-firing pearl stains: Rose, Aqua, Mint, and White.
- Three (3) "Touch-me" electronic music box buttons.
- Flat-back rhinestones.
- Ribbon.
- Glue.

Base coat all of the hearts with a mixture of two (2) parts of White and one (1) part of Smog Gray.

CHRISTMAS IS FRIENDS HEART:
Antique with a mixture of 1/2 teaspoonful of Holly Brite and a full jar of Lime Lite. Drybrush Mint on the background of the heart, slowly building up the color. Highlight this same area with Flesh, using a little more Flesh in the creases at the edge of the heart. Drybrush White on the lace. Thin a little Spring Green and paint the holly leaves, then apply two (2) coats of Mint pearl over them. Paint the berries with White pearl.

CHRISTMAS IS LOVE HEART:
Antique with Pink Crystal. Drybrush the background of the heart with Rose and highlight it with Flesh, using a little more of the Flesh in the creases. Drybrush White on the lace. Thin a little Plum and paint the holly leaves, then apply two (2) coats of Rose pearl over them. Paint the berries with White pearl.

CHRISTMAS IS FAMILY HEART:
Antique with Aqua Sheen. Drybrush the background of the heart with Turquoise. Highlight with Flesh, using a little more Flesh in the creases. Drybrush White on the lace. Thin a little Peacock and paint the holly leaves, then apply two (2) coats of Aqua pearl over them. Paint the berries with White pearl.

If you wish to add a little extra sparkle to the hearts, glue flat-back crystal rhinestones around the base of the lace on each one.

Glue the "Touch-me" electronic music box buttons into the hole in the back of each heart. ∎

Easter Eggs

MATERIALS LIST:

- ☐ Non-firing opaque stains: White, Smog Gray, Buttercup, Blond, Flesh, Ginger, Moss, and Rose.
- ☐ Non-firing translucent stains: Peach-glo and Pink Crystal.
- ☐ Ribbon.
- ☐ Two (2) "Touch-me" electronic music box buttons.

Base coat both eggs with a mixture of two (2) parts of White and one (1) part of Smog Gray.

HAPPY EASTER EGG:

Antique with Peach-glo.
Drybrush White on the lace. Drybrush the front and back with Buttercup and highlight with Blond. Lightly highlight the wrinkles around the edge with Flesh.

Using a stylus, make center dots for the flowers with Ginger, then make five (5) dots of White around each one, forming a flower. Using a feature brush, make two (2) brush-print leaves on each side of the flowers with Moss. Paint tiny curved lines of Moss connecting each flower. Paint some dots of Ginger next to the curved lines.

LOVE AT EASTER EGG:

Antique with Pink Crystal.
Drybrush White on the lace. Drybrush Rose on the front and back of the egg, then lightly highlight with Flesh.

Using a stylus, make center dots of Rose for the flowers, then make five (5) dots of White around each one to form the flowers. Using a feature brush, paint two brush-print leaves on each side of the flowers with Moss. Paint tiny curved lines of Moss connecting the flowers. Scatter some dots of Rose next to the curved lines.

Tie the ribbon on each egg and glue in the "Touch-me" electronic music box button. ■

Baby Girl

MATERIALS LIST:

- Non-firing opaque stains: White, Smog Gray, Rose, Soft Pink, Flesh, and Moss.
- Non-firing translucent stain: Pink Crystal.
- Ribbon.
- Glue.
- "Touch-me" electronic music box button.
- Flat-back pearls (optional).

Base coat with a mixture of two (2) parts of White and one (1) part of Smog Gray. Antique with Pink Crystal.

Step 1: Drybrush Rose on the front and back. Highlight with Flesh on the creases and lightly on the wording.

Step 2: Drybrush White on the lace.

Step 3: Use a pencil to make a dot for the position of each flower center. Using a feature brush and Soft Pink, make five (5) brush print petals around each dot (see Drybrushing and Soft Sculpture Basics: XI). Make the center dots Rose. Use Moss for the leaves and vines. Paint tiny White dots at random between the flowers.

Step 4: Tie on the ribbon.

Step 5: Glue the "Touch-me" music box button into the opening in the back of the piece.

Step 6: If desired, glue flat-back pearls around the base of the lace. ■

Baby Boy

MATERIALS LIST:

- Non-firing opaque stains: White, Smog Gray, Copenhagen, Baby Blue, Flesh, and Moss.
- Non-firing translucent stain: Golden Dusk.
- Ribbon.
- Glue.
- Flat-back pearls.
- "Touch-me" electronic music box button.

Base coat with a mixture of two (2) parts of White and one (1) part of Smog Gray. Antique with Golden Dusk.

TO PAGE 49

Happy Father's Day

MATERIALS LIST:
- Non-firing opaque stains: White, Smog Gray, Butterscotch, Camel, Flesh, Moss, and Russet.
- Non-firing translucent stain: Copper Oak.
- Flat-back pearls (optional).
- Glue.
- Ribbon.
- "Touch-me" electronic music box button.

Base coat with a mixture of two (2) parts of White and one (1) part of Smog Gray. antique with Copper Oak.

Step 1: Drybrush Butterscotch on the front and back of the piece. Highlight around the creases with Camel and then lightly with Flesh.

Step 2: Drybrush White on the lace, building up the color slowly.

Step 3: Use a pencil to make a dot to make the position for the center of each flower. Using a feature brush and Camel, make brush-print petals around each dot (see Drybrushing and Soft Sculpture Basics: XI). Make the center dots russet. Use Moss for the leaves and veins. Paint tiny White dots at random between the flowers.

Step 4: Tie the bow through the little hole in the lace.

Step 5: Glue the "Touch-me" music box button into the opening in the back of the piece.

Step 6: If desired, glue flat-back pearls around the base of the lace. ■

Happy Mother's Day

MATERIAL LIST:
- Non-firing opaque stains: White, Smog Gray, Moss, Ginger, Rose, Melon Pumpkin, and Flesh.
- Non-firing translucent stain: Peach-glo.
- Ribbon.
- Glue.
- Flat-back pearls.
- "Touch-me" electronic music box button.

Base coat with a mixture of two (2) parts of White and one (1) part of Smog Gray. Antique with Peach-glo.

Step 1: Drybrush Ginger on the front and back panels. With the Ginger still on the brush, tip into Flesh and highlight around the creases and across the wording.

Step 2: Drybrush White on the lace.

Step 3: Use a pencil to mark a dot for the location of each flower center. To make a light peach color for the flowers, mix together 1 teaspoonful of White, 1/2 teaspoonful of Pumpkin, and 1 1/2 teaspoonfuls of Rose. Using a feature brush and the light peach mixture, make brush-print petals around each center dot (see Drybrushing and Soft Sculpture Basics: XI). For the center dots of the flowers, use a mixture of one (1) part Melon and two (2) parts of Ginger. Use Moss for the leaves and vines. Paint tiny White dots at random between the flowers.

Step 4: Tie on the ribbon.

Step 5: Glue the "Touch-me" music box button into the opening in the back of the piece.

Step 6: If desired, glue flat-back pearls around the base of the lace. ■

Birthday and Wedding Wishes

MATERIALS LIST:
- Non-firing opaque stains: White, Smog Gray, Camel, Flesh, and Moss.
- Non-firing translucent stain: Golden Fawn.
- Non-firing pearl stains: Rose and Aqua.
- Flat-back pearls.
- Glue.
- Two (2) "Touch-me" electronic music box buttons.

Base coat both hearts with a mixture of two (2) parts of White to one (1) part of Smog Gray. Antique with Golden Fawn.

Step 1: Drybrush Flesh on the lace and highlight with White. Drybrush Camel on the center part and highlight with Flesh on the wrinkles around the edges.

Step 2: As a guide, make a dot with a pencil where each flower is to be placed. Paint the petals with Flesh. Paint two leaves on each side of the flowers with Moss. Make the center dots on the wedding heart Rose pearl and the center dots on the birthday heart Aqua pearl. Scatter White dots between the flowers.

Step 3: Glue flat-back pearls around the base of the lace.

Step 4: Tie on the bows.

Step 5: Glue in the "Touch-me" music box buttons. ∎

BABY BOY
FROM PAGE 45

Step 1: Mix together two (2) parts of Baby Blue and one (1) part of Copenhagen. Drybrush the front and back panels with the blue mixture. Highlight with Flesh on the creases and across the wording.

Step 2: Drybrush White on the lace.

Step 3 Use a pencil to mark a dot for the position of each flower center. Using a feature brush, make brush-print petals of Baby Blue around each center dot. Use Copenhagen for the center dots. Make the leaves and vines Moss. Make tiny White dots at random between the flowers.

Step 4: Tie on the ribbon.

Step 5: Glue the "Touch-me" music box button into the opening in the back of the piece.

Step 6: If desired, glue flat-back pearls around the base of the lace. ∎

The brushes used for the projects in this book are by Stangren; the styluses are by Kemper Mfg., Inc. and Duncan Ceramic Products; the stains mentioned are by Studio Stain; and the molds are by Dona's Molds.

Notes:

Notes:

Other Books by Dona Snipes:

Drybrushing with Dona by Dona Snipes. One of our best sellers! An 8½" × 11", 48 page FULL-COLOR book, written and profusely illustrated by one of the nation's top drybrush decorators, sharing all of her secrets.

Magnets by Dona Snipes. Make a set of magnets for a great gift and bazaar item. Features complete drybrushing instructions. Techniques are suitable for use on larger projects of similar design. A "handy" size format & best seller.

Available From:

Scott PUBLICATIONS

Credit Card Orders Call Toll Free:
For Speed & Convenience
1-800-458-8237

30595 W. 8 MILE RD.
LIVONIA, MICH 48152
313/477-6650